Martin Kluger

The Fugger Dynasty in Augsburg

Merchants, Mining Entrepreneurs, Bankers and Benefactors

context verlag Augsburg
www.context-mv.de

Martin Kluger

The Fugger Dynasty in Augsburg

Merchants, Mining Entrepreneurs, Bankers and Benefactors

Editorial Information

The Fugger Dynasty in Augsburg,
Merchants, Mining Entrepreneurs,
Bankers and Benefactors

Martin Kluger
context verlag Augsburg
ISBN 978-3-939645-74-0
1st edition, March 2014

Publisher:
Regio Augsburg Tourismus GmbH

Graphics and production:
concret WA GmbH, Augsburg

Bibliographical Information:
The German National Library

The German National Library
lists this publication in the
German National Bibliography,
for detailed bibliographical information visit: http://dnb.ddb.de

ISBN 978-3-939645-74-0

Contents

The Fugger Dynasty from 1397 to the present day—a short history

HINTERE GASSE

Jakob Fugger the Rich founded the Fuggerei. The rent for the residents: 0.88 euros per year and three prayers every day for the benefactor.

Fabulously rich—even today the Age of the Fuggers is still talked about

It is almost impossible to imagine the incredible wealth of the business magnates Jakob and Anton Fugger and the enormous power it gave them. It has been speculated that, when compared with present day circumstances, the Fugger undertaking at the pinnacle of its power was the most important company in the world, with no other business coming anywhere near it. Never before and even after the Fugger dynasty, has any single "company" had such enormous economic power and political influence. It is also said that no other entrepreneur has ever been as rich as the merchant Anton Fugger of Augsburg. Only once in the history of the world has an epoch been named after a mercantile company, still known today as "The Age of the Fuggers".

Diminishing yields from mining together with the shifting of political and geographic boundaries, major changes in the trading routes and the confusion arising from the Thirty Years' War brought an end to the Fugger undertakings. The business however, never actually went bankrupt. Forward-looking investments in assets such as castles, residences, land and art have ensured that the descendants, although no longer immensely wealthy, continue to count amongst the leading families of Germany, up to the present day.

The Augsburg merchant Jakob Fugger created the oldest existing social settlement in the world.

Fountain in Augsburg with the figure of Augustus, the founder of the city. A stone memorial in the Roman Museum reminds us of the trading route from Rome.

The former Roman Road paved the way for the rise of the Fugger family

When Jakob Fugger crossed the Alps in order to serve his apprenticeship in Rome and Venice, he followed the route on which the Roman legions had marched: Via Claudia. This military and trade route in the "splendissima Raetiae provinciae colonia", the splendid provincial capital Raetiae, today known as Augsburg, was the fastest and best way to cross the Alps right up until the last century. 1400 years after construction of this route, in the Late Middle Ages, the merchants of Augsburg once again profited from the connection with economically prosperous Italy. In the 14th century, trading had made Augsburg the place of transshipment between the centers of trade in Northern Italy, Flanders, the Hanseatic League and wealthy city of Nuremberg.

However, it was not until the meteoric rise of the Fuggers (Hans Fugger, the patriarch of the family, migrated here in 1367) and the old-established Welsers that the way was paved for Augsburg to become the leading financial metropolis in the Europe of the Early New Age and the showplace for the glorious days of the Empire. The rich city of Augsburg became the favourite place, where Emperor Maximilian I von Habsburg chose to stay, thus becoming a center for both political decision-making and also for culture and the arts.

Its location close to the Alps made Augsburg an important town for trade.

Jakob Fugger controlled his business empire from his office, the "Goldene Schreibstube" (Golden Writing Room). Bust of Jakob Fugger in the Fuerst Fugger Private Bank.

Jakob Fugger was the outstanding **financial genius** of the Renaissance

Jakob Fugger financed the rise to power and the imperial crown of the Habsburgs. He minted coins for the popes and paid their Swiss Guard. On the basis of the "family business" which had grown over only three generations, and with mercantile knowledge from Italy, with the benevolence of the Habsburg Maximilian I, with the "black gold" of the Prince-Bishop of Bressanone (Brixen) and silver and copper from Tyrol and Hungarian ore mines, he created a mining, banking and trading corporation. His commercial empire extended from the North Sea to the Adriatic, from the Atlantic Ocean to far beyond Eastern Europe. In 1493, there were even negotiations about a China expedition; in 1505-1506 Fugger participated in the first German trade journey to India; in 1525 he financed Sebastian Cabot's expedition to the New World. Jakob Fugger almost single-handedly raised the money to literally buy the votes from those electors who in 1519 then elected the Spanish King Charles, the grandson of Emperor Maximilian I, to Emperor Charles V.

His most outstanding monument is the Fuggerei in Augsburg, a social housing foundation, today 500 years old and the oldest almshouses in the world. The financial genius of the Renaissance also gave his name to the Fugger Chapel and the Fugger houses in Augsburg.

In 1476, the Fugger family became the banking house of the popes. Up until 1524 they minted papal coins.

Albrecht Dürer designed plans for the Fugger Chapel in the Church of St. Anna. The artist from Nuremberg is also thought to have been involved in the design of the Fuggerei.

Fugger and Dürer: The master of finance and the master of art

It is still true today that Albrecht Dürer is the most well-known German artist outside Germany. The close connections that the Fugger family had with this genius are not so well-known. For example from 1505 to 1507 the Fugger family financed Dürer's stay in Venice. During this time he painted "La Fête du Rosaire", possibly commissioned by Jakob Fugger, for the Church of the German Merchants at the Rialto. The altar painting shows Mary with the Christ Child surrounded by the powerful figures of the world.

In 1520, Dürer created the impressive portrait of Jakob Fugger which today is a highlight in the State Art Gallery of Old German Masters in the Schaezler Palais. In 1518, during the time of the Reichstag (Diet) in Augsburg, Dürer painted the portrait of the Emperor Maximilian I von Habsburg. It was Dürer who also designed the tomb funded by Jakob Fugger in the Church of St. Anna and it is said that he also gave advice to the Augsburg business magnate during the construction of the Fuggerei. At the same time the Fuggers earned quite a lot of money from Dürer's works of art. Their trading posts throughout Europe handled the demand for the engravings by the artist from Nuremberg.

Jakob Fugger the Rich, painted by Albrecht Dürer. Commissioned by this rich Augsburg merchant, Dürer also painted the portrait of Emperor Maximilian I in Augsburg.

Putto in the Fugger Chapel (above) and the Apostles before one of the four Fugger tombs in the St. Ulrich Basilica in Augsburg.

Burial tombs and the Ladies' Courtyard: The Renaissance begins in Augsburg

Jakob Fugger the Rich was the top man of a huge corporation and had a modern way of thinking. The developments in science, technical innovations, money-lending with high interest charges, monopoly business and the give-and-take between him and the powerful men of the time were the basis for his business empire. During his apprenticeship in Rome and Venice, however, he had also learnt more than the power of capital, non-cash payment systems and double-entry bookkeeping: Jakob was also greatly impressed by artistic and architectural aspects of the Italian Renaissance.

Augsburg's enormously successful businessman was in a position to commission buildings in the new style. The Fugger Chapel designed by Dürer in the Church of St. Anna, the tomb of Jakob Fugger and his brothers Ulrich and Georg, was the first and at the same time the most perfect Renaissance structure in Germany: Leading artists created the Fugger Chancel, donated in 1506 and finished in 1512. Jakob's "Ladies' Courtyard" was the most splendid of four courtyards within the Fugger houses in Augsburg and the first non-sacred building in Germany in Renaissance style, followed decades later by the Fugger tombs and the Fugger castles, also in the style of the Renaissance.

Italian flair in the center of Augsburg: Jakob Fugger had the Ladies' Courtyard built in the Fugger houses, completed in 1515.

Jakob Fugger had the Fugger residences built from 1512 to 1515. His descendants extended this enormous city palace.

After his marriage, Jakob Fugger had the Fugger houses built

In 1498, Jakob Fugger, almost 40 years old, married the 18-year-old Sybilla Artzt and the rich merchant now looked for a suitable residence. Like many other things in the life of this financial genius, it took on great proportions. Jakob Fugger acquired several houses in the wine market of Augsburg, which he then had demolished. In their place a new Fugger house was erected from 1512 to 1515. In 1517 and in the decades to follow, Jakob and his successors bought further buildings and so the Fugger houses came into being as they can still be seen today. The most interesting of four courtyards is the Ladies' Courtyard, built in 1515. The Ladies' Courtyard and the Serenade Courtyard are open to the public (in contrast to many interesting relics of the city palace which were destroyed in World War II). The Princes' Hall (today the foyer of the Fuerst Fugger Private Bank) gives us an impression of the former grandeur.

An oriel in the Serenade Courtyard reminds us of Emperor Charles V. He resided in the splendid rooms behind the front. Famous guests at the Fugger houses were Maximilian I, the artist Titian and the Swedish King Gustav II Adolph, who all stayed here, where Mozart performed in concert. A memorial plaque on the front tells us that Martin Luther was interrogated by Cardinal Cajetan here in 1518.

In the tiltyard of the Augsburg Fugger residence.

In 1518, Luther was interrogated in the Fugger houses. During his time in Augsburg he stayed in the Carmelite Cloister of St. Anna.

The Reformer Martin **Luther** was Jakob Fugger's greatest critic

The conflict between the Reformer Martin Luther and Jakob Fugger was predestined. The Fuggers were bankers to the popes, they therefore also earned money from the sale of indulgences which Luther strongly opposed. Interest charges, the accumulation of capital and economic power were the pillars supporting the Fugger business empire. The eloquent monk from Wittenberg, this vehement man of God was extremely critical of this and posed the question: "How can it be the will of God or justifiable that in such a short time one man can become so rich that he has kings and emperors under his control?" The Emperor Charles V did all he could to support Fugger capital enterprises, as he of course also benefited from Fugger capital, but the uprisings amongst the ore mineworkers and then the wars amongst the peasant farmers which had come about as a result of the Reformation, all caused problems for the Fugger business.

Jakob Fugger wrote: "It is Luther in fact, who is the initiator and the cause of unrest, outrage and bloodshed—even if he wishes it had never happened, it is now too late." When Luther was interrogated in the Fugger houses in 1518, he stayed in the Carmelite Cloister of St. Anna, where in the church there, the Fugger family had had their tombs erected.

The splendid burial chapel of the Catholic Fugger family can be seen in the Protestant Church of St. Anna.

Residents of the Fuggerei returning from the Sunday service in the St. Mark Church, built in 1581 by the Fugger family for their social settlement.

The Fuggerei: Almshouses, a social settlement as a memorial to Jakob Fugger

On the one hand Jakob Fugger practiced modern management methods as the head of his group of companies and he was totally without scruples when it came to interest charges and monopoly business actually prohibited by the church, the political pressure of the system of indulgences and financing military campaigns. Nevertheless he also had a strong religious faith instilled in him from the Middle Ages and at this time of the pending Reformation, he remained a stalwart son of the Roman Church. "In praise of God and in gratitude for the mercantile success of the House of Fugger" he established a housing estate for citizens of Augsburg who had become poor through no fault of their own. The annual rent today is 88 cents (originally one Rhenish florin) together with three prayers every day for the souls of the family Fugger.

The Fuggerei, founded in 1521, is today a tourist magnet and a place of pilgrimage for architects. As in the 16th century, the settlement is financed by the earnings of the Fugger Foundation Fund. Circa 150 needy people of Augsburg live in 140 apartments in 67 houses. This "town within the town" has its own church, own entry gates and its own administration. Since 2006 the whole residential complex is a living museum. To the present day the Fuggerei is still managed by the Fugger Family Council.

About 200,000 paying visitors visit the Fuggerei every year.

Today in the Fondaco dei Tedeschi is the Post Office of Venice (above). Left: The monument to Ulrich Fugger on the Fugger house in Schwaz in Tyrol.

The Fugger Network: Trading posts, Fugger newspapers, places of discovery

At the time of Jakob Fugger, Nuremberg, Venice and Rome were the most important company subsidiaries. Here, as in many important trade and finance centers of Europe, were the Fugger "agencies" (a mixture of trading post, bank, horse stop, warehouse, post office and diplomatic representation).

When Columbus discovered America in 1492 and Vasco da Gama from Portugal discovered the sea route to India in 1498, the agencies in Antwerp and Lisbon gained in importance. After the Spanish King was elected Emperor Charles V, this gave rise to a number of agencies in Spain.

This is the reason that numerous traces of the Fugger enterprises can be found in many countries of Europe. In Nuremberg an epitaph to Peter Fugger was discovered on the north side of the Sebaldus Church which is the oldest representation of Jakob Fugger and his family (even if only as an allegory). In Venice we see the Fondaco dei Tedeschi at the Rialto, in Rome there is a Fugger Chapel, in the Cathedral of Antwerp the Fugger Window, in Spain a palace in Almagro and the Church Portal of San Blas. In Tyrol the Fugger houses in Schwaz and Sterzing, Tratzberg Castle and the "Devil's Palace" in Trento (Trient) bear witness to the Fugger company which, with its Fugger "newspapers" and couriers, maintained a network throughout Europe.

The epitaph of Peter Fugger on the Sebaldus Church in Nuremberg.

The Fuggers also traded in exotic plants of that time, such as the then very precious tulip. In Augsburg they founded a zoo, presumed to be the first in Germany.

Sea trade with India, tulips for the Netherlands and the first German zoo

Fugger money contributed to the exploration of the New World and to trade with India and Africa. In 1505, Jakob Fugger and the Welsers, together with other merchants from Augsburg and Nuremberg and with Italian business associates invested in a trading journey which had never been made before "as the first Germans to travel to India". The yields were high, as they also were later from trade with the West African Kingdom of Benin. In 1531, Anton Fugger secured a colonial lease agreement for Chile and parts of Peru from the Spanish monarchy. The Conquistadors Pizarro and Almagro beat the Swabians to it but they were nevertheless able to continue trade with South America.

The Augsburg merchants also had the benefit of their worldwide trading network: Hans Fugger brought animals from Africa and South America and founded what is said to be the first German zoo to which the public had access. The Fugger firm however, imported not only exotic animals but also rare plants from far away countries. Presumably they traded at a very early date in tulips from Turkey which at that time were enormously expensive. The Neptune Fountain at the Fuggerei is a reminder of their sea trade routes all over the world.

The Neptune Fountain outside the Fuggerei: When this was erected, the trading ships of the Fugger and Welser families were sailing over the oceans of the world.

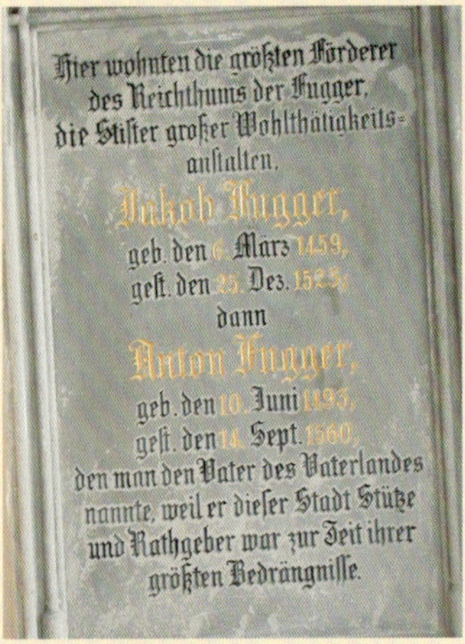

Anton Fugger (right) was the richest man of his time. A memorial plaque in the Fugger houses calls the savior of Augsburg "The Father of the Fatherland".

Jakob's nephew and successor Anton became the richest of the Fugger dynasty

For a long time there was a legend that Jakob Fugger had thrown the borrower's notes from the Emperor Charles V von Habsburg into the fire, but this really is only a nice story. A Fugger would never have burned these certificates of indebtedness! The truth is that the Emperor Charles V, whose brother, the German King and later Emperor Ferdinand I and their successors had such large debts with the Fugger family, that in the end the Habsburgs were simply unable to pay them back. The close relations with the Habsburg dynasty was the reason both for the rise to power and for the downfall of the Fugger business.

During the reign of Charles V, the Fugger group concern under Jakob Fugger's nephew and successor Anton Fugger reached the peak of its corporate assets in 1546. From 1545, the Fugger Bank provided huge credit sums to the Kings of England and also, after 1553, to Duke Cosimo I Medici of Florence, who had inherited the Italian banking house, which had long since been overshadowed by the Fugger bank. A contemporary called Anton "a true Prince of Merchants". In 1547, he saved Augsburg from destruction by kneeling before Emperor Charles V in Ulm after the Schmalkaldic War was lost, and was thereafter honored as "Father of the Fatherland".

A painting in the Princes' Hall of the Fuerst Fugger Private Bank shows Anton next to Emperor Charles V and Titian.

Left: A view of Kirchheim Castle, built by order of Hans Fugger.
Above: The Fugger Castle in Babenhausen.

The withdrawal from business to the country and to the castles

Little by little, Anton Fugger began to convert the company capital into land ownership, property and art. The economic downfall of Habsburg realm could be easily foreseen, the constant demands for credit on the part of kings and emperors was becoming a cause for worry: Three Spanish state bankruptcies were to cost the Fugger firm unimaginably high sums. Another problem too, was the lack of any suitable successor in the family to take control of the business.

So for these reasons, and because the heirs wanted to enjoy life, the Fugger family gradually withdrew from Augsburg which at the time was embroiled in religious disputes and from the major fields of business which had become politically and economically uncertain.
In 1538, Anton Fugger acquired Babenhausen where he had a castle built (1541-1543). The richest merchant in the world was laid to rest in the castle church of Babenhausen. There has been a Fugger Museum in the castle since 1955. From 1578 to 1585, Anton's son Hans Fugger built the Castle of Kirchheim, including the impressive Cedar Hall, one of Germany's most beautiful Renaissance interiors. These two castles in the Allgaeu region are open to visitors. Babenhausen and Kirchheim are only about an hour's drive away from Augsburg.

The wood of the cedar of Lebanon gave its name to the magnificent Cedar Hall in Kirchheim Castle.

The Hercules Fountain and the Mercury Fountain were created by Adriaen de Vries during the time that the Town Curator Octavian Secundus Fugger was in office.

A monument and two fountains thanks to the Fugger family's love of the arts

In the whole of Augsburg there is only one Fugger monument and this was commissioned by a Bavarian king: The over-dimensional bronze figure of Hans Jakob Fugger. The nephew of Anton Fugger with his eldest son Markus took over management of the Fugger company. However, because of very high personal debts, Hans Jakob withdrew from the company, left Augsburg and became Privy Councilor and Court Chamber President to Duke Albrecht V von Bayern. In 1571, he sold his precious collection of antique manuscripts and books to the Wittelsbach Duke. These now form the core section of the Bavarian State Library and for this reason, Ludwig I of Bavaria later donated the statue of Hans Jakob Fugger (in 1857).

The generations after Anton Fugger regarded themselves more like landed gentry, art collectors and patrons than as merchants and bankers. It is said that Markus Fugger's favorite saying was "I know of nothing more beautiful in the world than a beautiful lady and a beautiful horse." He wrote a classic manual about horse breeding. Octavian Secundus Fugger was a humanist and patron of music. The Mercury Fountain and Hercules Fountain were erected during his period of office as the town curator of Augsburg.

An over-dimensional bronze statue in honor of Hans Jakob Fugger was commissioned in 1857 by the Bavarian King.

Leopold Mozart attended a school financed by the Fuggers with the rococo salon as a memorial. (Left) His son played the Fugger organ.

The Fuggers, the Mozarts and a memorial plaque in the Fuggerei

Leopold Mozart as father and music teacher discovered the musical genius of his son. Leopold was born in Augsburg and underwent the training and music education which he passed on to Wolfgang Amadeus in the school of the Jesuit College which the Fuggers had founded in 1580. The Small Golden Salon reminds us of this. W. A. Mozart is also said to have had dealings with the Fuggers. In 1766, it was a member of the Fugger family who initiated an organ competition with a local child prodigy in the Church of the Fugger-owned Biberbach. In 1777, Mozart played the Fugger organ in the St. Ulrich Basilica in Augsburg and performed a concert in the Fugger house.

The paths of these two families had already crossed in previous generations. The three master builders in the Mozart family worked in the Fuggerei, on the Fugger houses or on a Fugger castle. The name David Mozart, the first Mozart ancestor in Augsburg appears in the bookkeeping records of the Fugger Foundation. In 1681, W. A. Mozart's great-grandfather Franz Mozart moved into the Fuggerei, the social settlement founded by Jakob Fugger for needy burghers of Augsburg. He was not forced by need to live there: He worked there as a master builder. Franz Mozart died in 1694 in the Fuggerei. There is a memorial plaque in the Fuggerei.

Franz Mozart lived and died in the Fuggerei.

Fugger coat of arms and precious stones in the Thekla Church in Welden (left). Above: The baroque church of pilgrimage in Biberbach then under Fugger rule.

The Fugger churches
are a celebration of baroque and rococo

Remembrances of the Fugger family can be found in numerous churches in Bavarian Swabia. In the 16th century the style of the Renaissance had left its mark on the burial tombs of the Fuggers in the Church of St. Anna in Augsburg and in the Ulrich Basilica and also in the churches of the Fugger Castles at Babenhausen and Kirchheim. The Fuggers also financed sacral buildings and ecclesiastical art in the Augsburg area and near their castles of Kirchberg, Babenhausen, Kirchheim, Markt, Glött, Laugna and Oberndorf. Visitors to these magnificent Fugger churches today are delighted with the baroque and rococo styles.

In Biberbach (Rural Administration District Augsburg) the connection between the worldly Fugger rule and at the same time their enthusiasm for baroque style churches can clearly be seen. When you look at it from the south, the slender tower of this church of pilgrimage rises before the dungeon of the former Fugger castle Markt. In the village church Kirchhaslach in Allgaeu, hardly anyone would expect the incredible wealth of paintings and figures which make this church a jewel of baroque. Joseph Maria Graf Fugger made a vow and founded the light-flooded Thekla Church in Welden, the most beautiful rococo church in the Augsburg area.

Joseph Maria Graf Fugger (left) was the benefactor of the Thekla Church in Welden. He can be seen on the founder's altar.

The Fugger coat of arms at the gateway to Oberkirchberg Castle (left). In Donauwoerth, the Fugger house dominates the main street (above).

Wherever you go in Swabia the Fuggers have already been there

In the political patchwork before the South German small states were done away with by Napoleon, the Fugger family was in possession of large areas of Swabia. The Fugger lily coat of arms can be found well beyond Augsburg, on the Bavarian side of the border as in the neighboring Baden Wurttemberg. In 1507, Jakob Fugger purchased the county of Kirchberg and rule in Weissenhorn. Today Oberkirchberg Castle is on the Baden-Wurttemberg side of the River Iller and the castle which Jakob Fugger built in Weissenhorn under Emperor Maximilian I lies in Bavaria. Building projects of the Fugger dynasty can be found throughout northern Swabia. The former Fugger castles, the Fugger houses in Dillingen on the Danube, in the main street of Donauwoerth give us an idea of the extent of the former land ownership.

In the Allgaeu region there is more to see than just the Fugger castles in Babenhausen and Kirchheim. In the Fugger Building in Memmingen, for example, Wallenstein and Gustav II Adolph of Sweden once resided. There is even a castle on the shores of Lake Constance and a typical Alpine "hut" with accommodation and grazing meadow in the lonely Allgaeu mountain valley near Hindelang which all bear traces of the Fugger family.

You will also come across evidence of the Fuggers in the Alps. They once bred noble horses in a valley near Bad Hindelang in Allgaeu.

The history of the Fugger Family

Migration, work and marriage: the rise of the House of Fugger

1367 to 1473: From the weaving mill to the dynamic Fugger firm

There are a lot of reasons for the founding of the city of Augsburg and why it is today known as the northernmost city of Italy. Rome in antiquity and in particular the Roman Emperor Augustus are responsible that Augsburg, located at the confluence of the Rivers Lech and Wertach, was first established as a camp for the Roman legions and later became known as "Augusta Vindelicum", the capital city in the Province of Raetiae. When the Alemannic peoples overran the Limes and the Danube, the Romans retreated back over the Alps.

As the Middle Ages gradually drew to a close, Augsburg was already the German gateway to Italy and as such was one of the most important towns to the north of the Alps. In this location it was a leading trade and banking center, far more important than for example, the cities of Frankfurt, Ulm, Luebeck, Regensburg, Strasburg and even Vienna. At the beginning of the 15th century, Augsburg stood alongside Cologne and Nuremberg with the highest population of any city in Germany. The "Golden

Above: Sebastian Münster's "Cosmographia" shows the location of Augsburg.

Age" of Augsburg began, when the "New World" was discovered and at the same time, when the Italian Renaissance created a new role for mankind in conjunction with a new understanding of the arts. A few decades later, Augsburg was compared with Florence and the Fugger dynasty was compared with the Medici. Renaissance Augsburg was extremely rich and very impressive. There was a poem which began with the line: "If only I had the power of Venice, the splendour of Augsburg...". The Italian humanist Aeneas Silvius Piccolomini wrote: "It is difficult to find something in another city which is better than in Augsburg."

This Roman milestone near Augsburg commemorates the Via Claudia Augusta.

There are a number of reasons for Augsburg's rise to importance: One reason was the geographic location of Augsburg which was on the Roman route, the Via Claudia, the Roman military and trading route to the River Danube, built by the Romans in 46 AD. At the time it was rather more a path than a road as we know it today, but it was to become the most important traffic route between Germany and Italy.

The short distance from Augsburg to Venice

This road connected Augsburg with Venice and was therefore a significant factor in the rise to power of Augsburg at the time of transition from the Middle Ages to the New Age, enabling Augsburg to become the finance center of Europe. The former Roman road brought trade and therefore also brought with it money, information and innovation. It also meant contact with the then superior mercantile know-how of northern Italy, for example, double entry bookkeeping, credit and interest charges and of course cashless financial transactions.

At that time, a journey from Augsburg to Venice in good weather took "only" ten days. The "Queen of the Seas" in the 15th century was the

center of world trade as well as being the rich and powerful bridge to the Levant and Arabia.

Silver mining made Germany rich

As well as the advantageous location of Augsburg was also the fact that all branches of business at that time were experiencing a dynamic upswing. In terms of silver mining, Germany was the European leader from 1470 to 1630. Silver and other ores were mined for example in Tyrol, in Austria, in the ore mining regions of Germany and Hungarian Slovakia. New technical systems had revolutionized mining; cog wheel and conveyor systems, stamping mills and metal-smiths all served to increase metal production. Looms were also improved. Printing with movable letters was invented around 1450. Important advances in shipbuilding technology and developments in compass and sextant systems arose through necessity during sea trade and the urge of exploration.

Upper Germany (reaching from Austria to Alsace, from Franconia to Switzerland) was a booming industrial center of the Holy Roman Empire of the German Nation. Money from Ulm was a reality, the Ravensburg Society was well funded for a long time, and towns like Memmingen or Noerdlingen were important centers of trade. Before

it was overtaken by Augsburg, the city of Nuremberg which lay at the junction of a number of trade routes, was the richest of the proud Free Imperial States.

"The Splendour of Augsburg": The trading town in the late Middle Ages. The beauty of Augsburg was proverbial at this time.

Augsburg: "Fucker advenit" in 1367

In 1367, Hans Fugger, "Hans the Weaver", the grandfather of the child who was later to be known as a financial genius, came from Graben to Augsburg in order to become a citizen of Augsburg. "Fucker advenit" (Fugger arrives) is entered in the tax records. The "city air" not only enabled Hans Fugger to be free but also to make his fortune.

The restless Fugger, who was not a poor man, married his first wife, the daughter of a Guild Weavers' Master (as was also his second wife). Master craftsmanship and marriage, both provided a sound monetary basis: Hans Fugger bought a house, became Master of the Guild and Alderman. In 1396, he was already at place 41 on the list of Augsburg's major taxpayers.

One of his sons was Jakob the Elder, the progenitor of the Fugger descendants "Fugger of the Lily". He had already trained as a goldsmith

Jakob Fugger the Elder (left). His son Peter Fugger died in 1473 in Nuremberg. His gravestone was set into the north wall of the St. Sebaldus Church.

and became a merchant. He also did not marry a poor woman: His wife became Barbara Baesinger, the daughter of a goldsmith, master of coin minting and dealer in silver. He married into the know-how from which later the whole of the Fugger group of companies was able to profit. There was already capital available: Eight years before his death, the father of the financial wizard Jakob Fugger (the Rich) was listed under the twelve richest burghers of Augsburg.

Jakob Fugger—the family's youngest son

This Jakob Fugger was born in 1459. He was the latecomer, the tenth of eleven children in the Fugger family. At the young age of 12 he was conferred a minor order of St. Vitus' in Herrieden of Central Franconia. But although Jakob Fugger received a clerical ordination, it had been decided at an early age that he would pursue the occupation of a merchant. At the latest in 1473 he began the necessary apprenticeship in Venice.

Jakob's eldest brother Ulrich was definitely the boss. Georg was responsible for business in Venice. Peter was head of the accounting office in Nuremberg. Markus was secretary in the papal offices in

Rome: An excellent basis for future business of the Fugger firm with the Curia. The Fugger "company" had already acted as banking house for the popes since 1476.

The blue and gold Fugger lilies can be seen on two of the gates of a former Fugger house in Augsburg which belonged to Ulrich and Jakob Fugger as of 1488.

Ulrich Fugger and the lily coat of arms

Three years previous, in 1473 in Augsburg, Ulrich Fugger had saved the Emperor Frederick III and his son Maximilian from a financial crisis. He provided this Habsburg family, which did not have the financial means, and their court escorts with all the fabric and accoutrements necessary to negotiate for a suitable bride. The Fugger family was then granted the lily coat of arms in gratitude for services rendered. It was also the subsequent fate of the Habsburg dynasty, which was later to influence the rise of the Fugger family.

Lithic Fugger lilies can be found in the Fuggerei, the oldest existing social settlement in the world today.

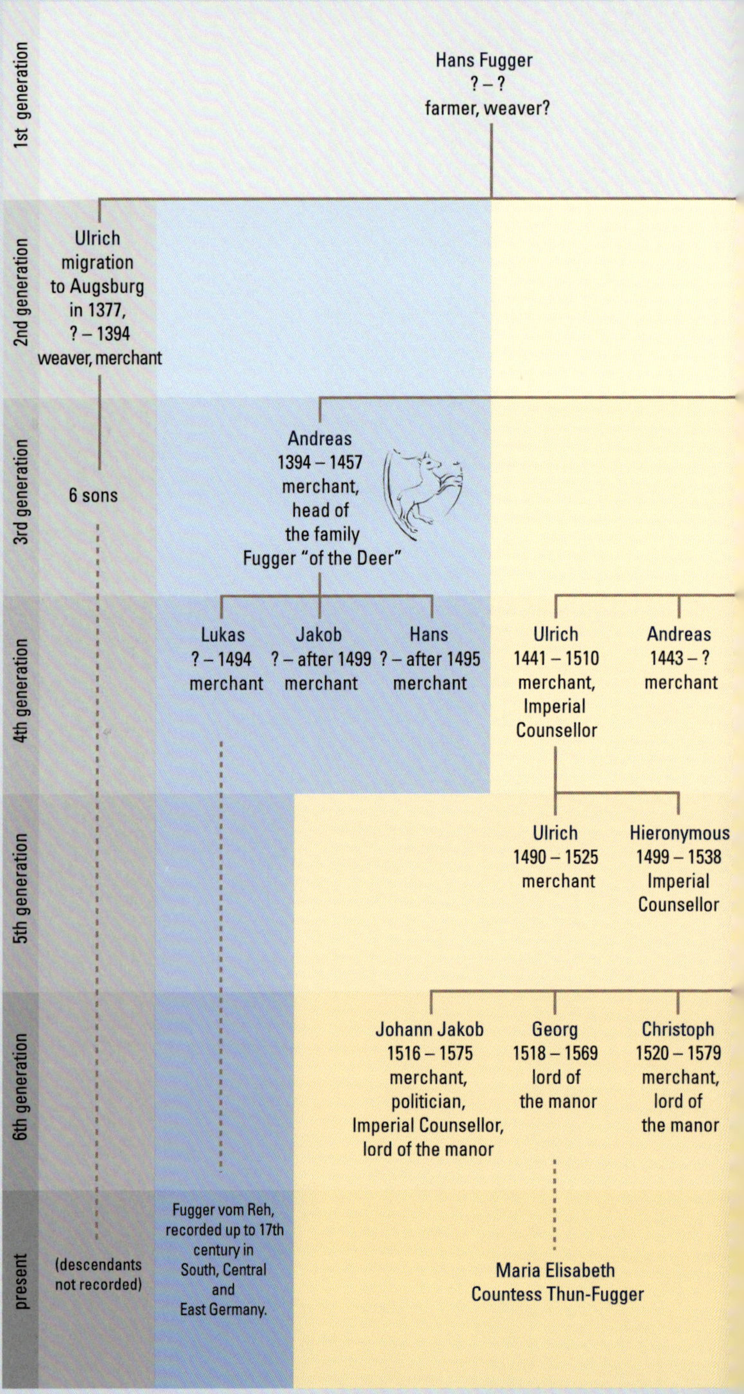
1st generation
Hans Fugger
? – ?
farmer, weaver?
2nd generation
Ulrich
migration
to Augsburg
in 1377,
? – 1394
weaver, merchant
3rd generation
6 sons
Andreas
1394 – 1457
merchant,
head of
the family
Fugger "of the Deer"
4th generation
Lukas
? – 1494
merchant
Jakob
? – after 1499
merchant
Hans
? – after 1495
merchant
Ulrich
1441 – 1510
merchant,
Imperial
Counsellor
Andreas
1443 – ?
merchant
5th generation
Ulrich
1490 – 1525
merchant
Hieronymous
1499 – 1538
Imperial
Counsellor
6th generation
Johann Jakob
1516 – 1575
merchant,
politician,
Imperial Counsellor,
lord of the manor
Georg
1518 – 1569
lord of
the manor
Christoph
1520 – 1579
merchant,
lord of
the manor
present
(descendants
not recorded)
Fugger vom Reh,
recorded up to 17th
century in
South, Central
and
East Germany.
Maria Elisabeth
Countess Thun-Fugger

Hans
migration to Augsburg in 1367
? – 1408/1409
master weaver,
alderman, merchant

Jakob the Elder
after 1398 – 1469
master weaver,
alderman, merchant,
head of the family
Fugger "of the Lily"

Hans
1445 – 1461
merchant

Markus
1448 – 1478
provost
Curia

Peter
1450 – 1473
merchant

Georg
1453 – 1506
merchant

Jakob the Rich
1459 – 1525
merchant,
Imperial Counsellor,
Imperial Count

Markus
1488 – 1511
cathedral
provost

Raymund
1489 – 1535
merchant,
Imperial Counsellor,
lord of the manor

Anton
1493 – 1560
merchant,
Imperial Counsellor,
lord of the manor

Ulrich
1526 – 1584
academic

Raymund
1528 – 1569
lord of
the manor

Markus
1529 – 1597
merchant,
alderman,
lord of
the manor

Johannes
1531 – 1598
merchant,
lord of
the manor

Hieronymous
1533 – 1573
lived on
private means

Jakob
1542 – 1598
lord of
the manor

Albert
Count Fugger von Gloett

Hubertus
Prince Fugger-
Babenhausen

Beginning of Career in Venice, silver from Tyrol, spices from East India

From 1473 to 1506: The unstoppable rise of Jakob Fugger

A document first recognized only a few years ago provides evidence that Jakob Fugger already resided in Venice at the age of 14 to receive his education as a merchant. Jakob was not the only person from Augsburg to be attracted to Venice. At this time it was usual for young people from Germany to go to Venice, Italy, to serve an apprenticeship: Italy was known to have the best commercial skills. In Venice there were 44 banks and 77 goldsmiths. Its port made this "The Queen of the Seas".

The young Jakob completed his apprenticeship in the "Fondaco dei Tedeschi", the House of German Merchants in Venice. Here he learned the advantages of double-entry bookkeeping, which at that time was practically unknown in Germany, and he studied the Italian monetary economy: bank transactions via a current account, bills of exchange and deposit receipts.

Before the new sea routes were discovered, Venice was the leading trade metropolis of Europe. Here Jakob Fugger began his career training as a merchant in 1473.

By 1478, four of Jakob's older brothers had died: Andreas (the year of his death is not known), Hans (1461 in Venice), Peter (1473 in Nuremberg) and Markus (1478 in Rome). At this time the Fugger family did not yet belong to the leading trading families of Augsburg, which had meanwhile become rich through trade with Italy, the center of trade for Europe. Jakob Fugger spent most of his time in Venice up to 1487; then, he returned to Augsburg where he began managing the firm more and more although it was still officially named after his older brother Ulrich. The rapid rise of the Fugger enterprise began.

In 1484, the Fuggers were given their own chambers in the Fondaco dei Tedeschi, founded in 1288—a clear confirmation of the growing importance of the Fugger firm for trade with Venice. In Venice, Jakob Fugger also experienced the spirit and arts of the Renaissance. This can be seen later in the buildings he commissioned in Augsburg, such as the Fugger Chapel, the Fugger Houses and the Ladies' Court. The Augsburg Fuggerei was also developed in accordance with examples of social housing which Jakob Fugger discovered in Venice.

In Venice: The Fondaco in Flames

Before the ports of Lisbon and Antwerp gained in importance, the Fondaco was the most important factoring office of the Fuggers. When in 1505 the House of German Merchants went up in flames (possibly arson, this is not known exactly), Jakob Fugger

The Fuggers' factory in Venice was located in the Fondaco dei Tedeschi.

A portrait of Jakob Fugger painted by Albrecht Dürer is presently displayed in the State Gallery of Old German Masters in Augsburg.

encouraged his initially indecisive colleagues to rebuild. The Fondaco was rebuilt with donations from German commercial enterprises.

In 1506, commissioned by Fugger, Dürer painted the "Fête du Rosaire" for the Church of German Merchants in Venice. This altar painting for the San Bartolomeo di Rialto Church shows the Pope, the Emperor and great men of the time, and possibly also (the experts are not in agreement) Georg Fugger, an older brother of Jakob. It has even been speculated that in this painting, the Madonna shows Jakob Fugger's wife Sybilla. In January 1498 the almost 40-year-old Jakob Fugger had married the 18-year-old Sybilla Artzt, the daughter of an Augsburg patrician family. The marriage remained childless and it is thought that it was not a very happy marriage. In 1526, a few weeks after Jakob Fugger's death, his widow Sybilla married again in unseemly haste.

The intervention of Jakob Fugger in European History

Since 1485 the Fuggers had managed their business in Tyrol from Innsbruck. Jakob Fugger was responsible for this important trading post and soon managed the entire and most important north-south trade route to Venice and Rome. In Tyrol at the age of 26, this man from Augsburg brought about his master stroke. On 5th December

1485 he came to do business for a comparatively low credit sum to the amount of 3,000 florins with the landowner of Tyrol, Archduke Sigmund, known as "rich in coins". Sigmund was extremely popular with the people of Tyrol but after his two marriages, the Habsburger remained without child even though it is said that he had more than 50 illegitimate descendants! Unfortunately the costs of holding court far exceeded his income and therefore Sigmund had considerable debts with the Bavarian banker Hans Baumgartner and the Wittelsbach Duke Albrecht IV. When in 1487 the childless Sigmund found himself in financial difficulty, he transferred his legal succession in Tyrol and now suddenly the 29-year-old Jakob Fugger entered major European politics. In 1488, he loaned Sigmund 150,000 florins, guaranteed by Tyrol silver production. When the right time came, Fugger then axed funds to the cash-strapped Archduke. The political plot was successful: In March 1490 Sigmund abdicated and declared his successor to the throne to be his relation, King Maximilian I.

Jakob Fugger, the "political banker"

Jakob Fugger now came onto the scene as "political banker" and for the first time he united the interests of the Fugger firm with the House of Habsburg. Jakob Fugger of Augsburg got on extremely well with Maximilian I, the sole

The Fugger House in Schwaz: In Tyrol the Fugger firm mined silver and copper until 1657.

In 1505/06, the Fuggers provided credit to finance the recruitment of the pontifical Swiss Guard which still exists today. Shortly thereafter gratitude was shown: Beginning in1508 the Fugger factory in Rome minted coins for four popes.

reigning monarch since 1493 (they were both at the same age). Occasionally the Habsburgs tried to free themselves from the strait jacket imposed by Fugger credit arrangements. The King and his banker were mutually dependent on each other.

In terms of banking: In 1486, the Council of the Imperial City of Augsburg mentioned for the first time the bank of Ulrich Fugger. Since 1500 the Fuggers had already been involved with the administrative management of papal indulgences throughout large areas of Germany, in France and Flanders, Scotland, Poland and Hungary. In 1476, they had already also been involved with other Curia transactions.

Im Rome: Bankers to the popes

At that time it was Jakob's brother Markus who had acted "somewhere in-between business and church", later his nephew of the same name, his successor (son of Georg Fugger who died in 1511 in Rome), followed by the factoring agent Johannes Zink.

Since the year 1500 the Fuggers were in charge of indulgency monies, in 1508 they took over the minting of coins. Sixty-six coins were minted under four popes and all bear the trademark of Fugger, the trident and ring. In 1505/06 the Fuggers also financed the establishment of the Swiss Guard for the popes. The Fugger firm still carried on with the original business–the textile trade. Fabrics were sold not only in Germany but also to Italy, the Netherlands, France, England and Portugal.

The real rise to power however, was in the field of ore mining, through trading and processing of metals. In only a few years the Fuggers built up a worldwide mining business: Silver and copper were mined in Tyrol, also in Thuringia, in the ore mines of Bohemia and Saxony, in the Mansfeld region, in Carinthia and most of all in the Slovakian ore mines (at that time belonging to Hungary). In 1494, the Fuggers engaged in trade with Hungary and began mining Hungarian copper and silver ores. Copper for example, was traded on the metal exchange in Venice or was processed in the form of artillery and cannonballs for Habsburg or papal troop defences.

The Fuggers in East India

After the discovery of the Americas and the ocean route to India, trading companies also enjoyed a significant boom. Until then, cotton and silk, spices and luxury goods from Italy were transported over Alpine passes and negotiations undertaken with the Hanse or Scandinavian merchants.

After 1503 the Fuggers also took part in the lucrative oriental spices trade. Together with merchants from Italy, Nuremberg and Augsburg, (e.g. the Welsers) the Fuggers invested in the risky trade journey from Lisbon to East India–"the first Germans to go to India". When the ships returned in 1506 there was 175 percent profit. This enterprise marked the beginning of German overseas trading.

In 1505 and 1506, the Fugger company participated in the first trading journey by sea undertaken by German merchants to East India.

Jakob Fugger: The great crisis and the buildings of the "Emperor-Maker"

1507 to 1525: The Fuggers pay for two imperial crowns

Despite their enormous financial success, the Fuggers were still deemed to be "nouveau riche" as far as the old Augsburg nobility was concerned. In 1498, the Fuggers were not even represented amongst the richest Augsburg citizens in the city tax records. At this time however, they were definitely on their way to the top.

A city and a castle for the bankers to the crown

As far as could be seen from outside the company, Ulrich Fugger still headed the business even though after the death of his brother Georg in 1506, it was Jakob Fugger who was de facto the boss of the company. One year later, in 1507, he purchased from Maximilian I for 50,000 florins the county of Kirchberg near Ulm including several villages and the town of Weissenhorn.

In 1509, Jakob Fugger "the Rich" founded the gorgeously designed Fugger chapel in the St. Anna Church in Augsburg.

The Habsburg ruler, until then "only" the German king, needed money in order to smooth the way in Rome to become emperor and be crowned as such. However,

Venice blocked his way to Rome. In 1508, Maximilian only got as far as Trento (Trient) on the southern border of his territories. Here the Habsburg king declared himself to be the "Chosen Roman Emperor". Jakob Fugger steadily acquired plots of land and thus gradually entered the nobility but he did not use his title as Count and continued to sign documents as "Fugger". When the Emperor Maximilian I then also wanted to be declared pope in 1511, even his good friend, the Augsburg banker, refused to provide any credit.

Fuggers threatened with bankruptcy

To the outside world the Fuggers continued to present themselves as a business family. From the comparatively small company capital however, there is no way that Jakob Fugger could have financed his business enterprises which were meanwhile spread throughout many parts of Europe: It was to be kept secret that in 1496 the Prince Bishop of Brixen (Bressanone), Cardinal Melchior von Meckau, invested immense sums, which he had received from mining interests, as silent partner in the Fugger firm.

On 5th March 1509 von Meckau died unexpectedly. His secret investment at this time represented three quarters of the total company capital. It suddenly became known and the Alpine Bishopric, the Emperor and the Pope were all in dispute over his inheritance. If the Fuggers had had to pay them out, then there is no doubt that the company would have gone bankrupt.

Instead Jakob Fugger came up with a masterpiece of tactical thinking: He played them all off against one another. In order to counter all rumours about his company's inability to pay, he instigated a successful public relations coup as if he had capital (at

Jakob Fugger is depicted on one of the two large organ wings in the Fugger chapel.

the time not available) purchasing power. From Maximilian I he now acquired lands in Schmiechen, which had been offered for some time. Jakob Fugger went even further: As of 1509 he had tombstones erected in the Anna Church for himself and his brother Ulrich, for which only the best (and therefore the most expensive) German artists of the time were commissioned, including Albrecht Dürer. And because Maximilian I could not relinquish his banker, he assisted him in the dispute with the pope. In the end Jakob Fugger was compared with the Curia. The pope was accepting—much to the advantage of the Fugger firm. The von Meckaus family and the bishopric of Brixen were left empty-handed.

Jakob Fugger builds his town palace

In the year 1510 a major crisis had been overcome, the year in which Jakob Fugger's elder brother Ulrich died at the age of 68. Jakob Fugger was now officially the head of the company. Although he drew up a new corporate agreement with his nephews Ulrich, Hieronymus, Raymund and Anton he was nevertheless the absolute ruler of the family concern. The new boss had up to now lived quite modestly, but then the time had come to show the outside world just how much purchasing power his company held.

From 1511 to 1515 Jakob Fugger commissioned the building of his Augsburg city palace. The Fugger Houses and the Ladies' Courtyard were designed in Renaissance style. These Fugger company headquarters impressed emperors, kings, princes and cardinals alike, a visual demonstration of the Fugger economic power by means of an imposing 68 meter long facade and a magnificent mix of classic German town house and Italian palace.

Castle and entombment

In 1512, the burial tombs for Ulrich, Georg and Jakob Fugger were finished by Dürer. The Fugger Chapel which forms the west chancel of the St. Anna Church was quite spectacular, not only because of the enormous expense involved; the Fugger Chancel is the most perfect construction of the German Renaissance. The Fugger Chapel was consecrated in 1518. Four years previously, in 1514, Jakob Fugger had acquired rulership of Biberbach and the Castle of Markt to the north of Augsburg, from the Emperor Maximilian I.

Up to 1515 Jakob Fugger's city palace was built. During this time the Damenhof (ladies' courtyard) was constructed.

This Habsburg ruler liked to be in town where he was popular amongst the people. He enjoyed being a guest of the Fugger family in the wealthy city of Augsburg. Here the emperor bought a house near the cathedral, a share of the Castle of Wellenburg to the south of Augsburg and a hunting castle in Mickhausen, also not far away. The emperor Maximilian I visited Augsburg on 17 official and private occasions. The city of Augsburg was at its peak of splendour and power and was a center of politics in Europe for several decades. Maximilian enjoyed life to the full: he spent two years and 211 days in Augsburg. In the French Court he was ridiculed for his love of Augsburg. There they called him "The Mayor of Augsburg".

Gold for Emperor Charles V

When Maximilian died in 1519, despite his political dallying he had nevertheless paved the way for the unification of Austria, Bohemia and Hungary. Jakob Fugger continued to place his faith in the Habsburg dynasty, even though this decision brought disadvantages to his relationship with both pope and Protestants, with kings and princes. After the death of Maximilian I, his grandson, the Spanish King Charles I was to be elected the new Emperor of the Holy Roman Empire of the German Nation and Jakob Fugger supported his candidature against

In order to clear debts, Charles V made the Fuggers beneficiaries of the mercury mines of Almadén. Jakob Fugger funded the St. Blas Church in Almagro in1525.

that of Pope Clemens VII and even the French King Franz I, favoured by a number of German princes.

When in 1519 Jakob Fugger provided a total of 852,000 florins for the election of Charles V as emperor. 544,000 florins were from him, 143,000 from the Augsburg House of Trade of the Welser family and the rest was from Italian financiers: Such figures bear witness to the enormous power of the Fuggers. These sums were needed to "encourage" the princes to vote for Charles V, in other words their votes were bought.

Repayment of this credit took a considerable time: In 1523, the merchant had to remind his imperial debtor of his excessive obligations and that redemption was due. Jakob Fugger sent him a written reminder which is unique in German history: "It is generally known and is quite obvious to all that Your Imperial Majesty would not have acquired the Roman Crown without me...". The result of this letter was: Fugger acquired the lucrative rights to Spanish mercury mines for his company.

Most of all however, Jakob Fugger was able to defend his company against the accusation brought in 1523 against six major South German companies, one of which was of course the Fugger concern, on the grounds of abuse of monopoly, exorbitant rates of interest and forcing

up prices. The Emperor was not able to defend the merchant against criticism from Martin Luther. The Reformer believed that "it is hardly possible for merchants to be without sin". He demanded that the Fuggers and other large business enterprises should be bridled.

Following the example of Venetian social housing, Jakob Fugger founded the Fuggerei in 1521, with construction beginning in 1516. Today the Fuggerei is the oldest social settlement in the world.

1521: The founding of the Fuggerei

Though his business was booming, Jakob Fugger gave thought to what was to happen after his death. He was concerned about a suitable successor from amongst his nephews but he was also concerned for his own soul. Already in 1516 Jakob Fugger had commissioned the building of terraced houses in the Jakob quarter of Augsburg for the benefit of respectable Augsburg burghers who had become needy through no fault of their own. In 1521, he signed the foundation certificate for what is today the oldest social settlement in the world.

The Fuggerei became a monument to Jakob Fugger. In private life unhappy, depressed by the religious disputes, the peasants' wars in Swabia, miners' strikes in Tyrol, Carinthia and Hungary and the dispute with the king of Hungary, Jakob Fugger died on 30th December 1525 at the age of 66.

N
W
O
S
Atlantic
London
Important bases
at the time of Anton Fugger
Overland trade routes
Sea routes
Cal
Nantes
Paris
Loire
Bordeaux
to India
Santander
Laredo
Bilbao
Villalón de Compos
Medina de Rioseco
Valladolid
Medina del Campo
Burgos
Segovia
Madrid
Toledo
Tejo
Tajo
Lisbon
Toulouse
Avigr
Narbonne
Saragossa
Barcelona
Almadén
Almagro
Valencia
Sevilla
Guadalquivir
Sanlúcar de Barrameda
Alicante
Cádiz
Granada
Malaga
to America
Mediterranean

North Sea
Baltic Sea
Adria
to Narwa
Helsingör
Copenhagen
Königsberg
Danzig
Elbing
Hamburg
Lübeck
Amsterdam
Lüneburg
Stettin
Thorn
Rhein
Antwerp
ruges
Braunschweig
Frankfurt
Posen
Cologne
Halle
Leipzig
Erfurt
Hohenkirchen
Breslau
Mainz
Frankfurt
Reichenbach
Kuttenberg
Neisse
Worms
Würzburg
Speyer
Prague
Freiwaldau
Krakow
Jablunkapass
Nuremberg
Neusohl
Kremnitz
Donauwörth
Regensburg
Straßburg
Ulm
Donau
Kaschau
Munich
Memmingen
Augsburg
Wasserburg
Linz
Pressburg
Basel
Rosenheim
Vienna
Lindau
Hall
Salzburg
Innsbruck
Schwaz
Buda
Pest
Lyon
Geneva
Brixen
Villach
to Russia
Bozen
Fuggerau
Ptuj
Trient
Milan
Verona
Treviso
Triest
Ljubljana
Zagreb
Vicenza
Venice
Genua
Padua
Topusko
Bologna
Rijeka
Senj
Marseille
Belgrade
Livorno
Florence
Ancona
Rome
Aquila
Naples
© context verlag Augsburg

At the **pinnacle** of wealth and the "gratitude of the House of Habsburg"

1526 to 1560: Anton Fugger becomes the richest man in the world

After his death, many people had many different things to say about Jakob Fugger—depending on their understanding of commerce, or their view of the world, their interests or their religious beliefs. For some people he was merely the deceased head of a company, and as such an exploiter, monopolist and usurer, whilst others held his indisputably superb performance in high esteem. The chronicler Clemens Sender wrote of him: "The pope greeted him like a dear son. The cardinals stood up in his presence ... and even the non-Christians admired him greatly." His epitaph in the Fugger tomb pays hommage to Jakob, the advisor to the Emperors Maximilian I and Charles V with the words: "Just as in his lifetime there was no-one to compare with him, now after his death there is no mortal to be found who can be compared with him."

After 1525 the mining of mercury in Spain was the most important segment of business of the Fugger enterprise. Among reminders of this time is the Fugger house in Almagro.

The figures speak for themselves: In the years after 1511, the company capital under Jakob Fugger was fourteen times greater and on average there was an annual profit of 76 percent. Jakob Fugger's nephew Anton as the new head of the company, therefore had to follow in great footsteps. A few days before his death, Jakob nominated the 32-year-old son of his brother Georg as his successor. For a long time this had not looked to be the case. Firstly it had been Ulrich Fugger, the son of Jakob's eldest brother Ulrich who was the favourite, but then he died in 1525 in Schwaz. Anton's elder brother Raymund could also have counted on his chances but failed on the grounds of his hot-headed temperament and his physical constitution. Raymund was then "only" responsible for administration of Fugger lands and properties.

The beginnings of company head Anton Fugger

Anton Fugger had already proven himself during a six-year stay in Rome where he was in charge of the problematic branch office there. He came to know the business under very difficult conditions. He also learned in Nuremberg, Breslau, Crakow, Vienna and Schwaz. As a 21-year-old Anton had already discovered embezzlement in the factoring office in Budapest and acted very quickly and independently to stop it.

Anton Fugger showed good form in managing the Fugger business during times which were becoming increasingly more difficult both in political and economic terms. Although in 1526 the court action against Fugger in respect of monopoly business was defeated, nevertheless in Hungary and Italy there were soon to be new causes for concern, shortly after he took over the company management. In 1525, it was Fugger money which decided the Battle of Pavia in favour of Emperor Charles V against the French who were allied with the Pope.

In the Santa Maria dell 'Anima Church in Rome, the Fuggers founded the Markus chapel. In one of the frescoes of this chapel Anton Fugger (far right) is said to be portrayed.

Emperor Charles V was the most important client of the Fugger banking house. Credit from Anton Fugger often saved his realm. This portrayal of the young emperor is imbedded in the facade of a house in Augsburg.

In 1527, Georg von Frundsberg from Mindelheim, the commander of the mercenary troops lost control of the situation. Following a stroke suffered by this "father of mercenaries", the hordes of mercenaries he had led were now without a leader and descended on Rome where it came to a terrible sacking "Sacco di Roma": men were murdered, women raped, cardinals savagely attacked. The Swiss Guard, financed by Jakob Fugger, enabled the Pope to take flight to the Engelsburg where they were slaughtered. Churches and palaces were plundered, precious works of art destroyed. The only safe place was in the Fugger agencies.

The end of the Fugger factory in Rome

Further, the Fugger factoring agent had silver mass utensils which had been stolen from the Cathedral of St. Peter and tableware from the Vatican melted down and made into coins, and also through him the mercenaries were able to transfer their spoils back to Germany. This marked the end of the Fugger Bank. Although Anton Fugger immediately dismissed his agent, it was nevertheless impossible to continue doing business there, particulary since the Pope, Clemens VII, was not a friend of the Germans anyway. The agency had to be closed.

The year 1526 saw the return of the Fugger firm ore mines in Hungary which had previously been confiscated. In no way did Anton Fugger forgive and forget that it was the Jagiellonen (then Polish) King Ludwig II, who in 1524 had spurned on the people of Budapest to a "People's Revolt" against the Fugger, in order to release himself in this way from his debts with the Augsburg family. When in 1526 the Hungarian nobleman Johann Zápolya joined forces with the Turkish Sultan Soliman as the leader of a rebellion against King Ludwig II, Anton Fugger gave his help only half-heartedly. He provided credit of only 50,000 florins when the King marched against the Turks who had invaded Hungary.

In 1527, Spanish and German troops attacked Rome. The pope fled to Castle of the Holy Angel (Castel Sant'Angelo). After the "Sacco di Roma," business between the Fuggers and the Curia was ended to the greatest extent.

On 29th August 1526 in the Battle of Mohács, the poorly armed Hungarian knights were subsequently defeated and King Ludwig II fell in battle. The Fugger firm ensured that the world discovered what the English courts and financial circles all thought at the time: This catastrophe could have been averted with the goodwill of the Fuggers.

The Fuggers and the Habsburg Crowns

In this way Anton Fugger influenced world history. That the Turks were able to besiege Vienna for the first time only three years later (also of course defended with the aid of Fugger money), was certainly not something that Fugger would have wished. At the same time however, the Augsburg Banker had interfered decisively in the quarrels over Hungary which lasted for decades. The Crown of Stephan now fell to the House of Habsburg. The basis for Austro-Hungarian dual monarchy which did not end until 1918 had been created with Fugger money.

The Fugger house in Neusohl is a reminder of Fugger mining in today's Slovakia.

In 1521, Archduke Ferdinand with the agreement of his elder brother, Emperor Charles V, became the ruler of Lower and Upper Austria, Styria, Kernten and Krain. In 1522, Charles V also handed Tyrol and West Austrian lands (Bavarian Swabia and parts of Wurttemberg) to his brother. Anton Fugger supported Ferdinand when the Habsburger was crowned King of Bohemia in February 1527 in Prague and in December 1527 then also acquired the Hungarian throne. When Ferdinand was subsequently chosen as King of the Holy Roman Empire of the German Nation in 1531, just as in 1519 for the election of Charles V, once again the Fugger financial power was needed to buy the votes from the Princes.

King Ferdinand I, who was to become the successor to Emperor Charles V in 1556, showed his gratitude to Anton Fugger, together with his brother Raymund and their cousin Hieronymus, by elevating them to the nobility. His relationship with the Augsburg banking house was nevertheless not good and remained as such.

Soon Anton Fugger's relations with Augsburg were also to deteriorate. In 1533, he had opposed an iconoclast assault by the Zwinglians in the Moritz Church and was condemned by the City Council of Augsburg to spend three days arrest in the tower on the grounds of insurrection. In July 1533, Anton Fugger withdrew to the Fugger weaving town of

In Antwerp the Fuggers maintained an extremely important factory. There, Anton Fugger (picture) and his cousin Hieronymus funded the Fugger window for the Cathedral of Our Lady. The glass painting portrays both donators.

Weissenhorn in great disappointment.

In these years business was good–not only the trade in fabrics from Weissenhorn, which were supplied even to England and Spain, but also copper and brass were exported to India and West Africa and trade with South America was good. The Fuggers only just missed out on becoming a colonial power in large parts of America: With the Spanish crown a colonial leasing agreement had been prepared in 1531, which was to assure the Fuggers Chile and Southern Peru. This huge area however was instead seized by the Conquistadors Pizarro and Almagro, who annexed the Inka realms by force. The factoring agency in Seville however, supplied fustian, copper, mercury as well as slaves to the New World.

Moreover, in his capacity as banker, Anton Fugger was able to assert great political influence, particularly via Antwerp and London. Credit facilities were provided to Charles V, to finance his campaigns against France and against the Turks, also to Ferdinand I, who fought in Hungary, to the King of England and to the Medici, who in 1532 became Dukes of Florence and in 1569 Grand Dukes of Tuscany. Anton Fugger appears to have taken the Medici as his role models: He ob-

Beginning in 1541, Anton Fugger contracted the construction of his favourite palace in Babenhausen. This palace is still in possession of Prince Fugger of Babenhausen today.

viously tried hard to achieve the creation of a Duchy of Swabia. He acquired lands in and around Mickhausen, Oberndorf, Gloett, Donauwoerth, Babenhausen and Kirchheim, Gablingen, Pless, Rettenbach and west of the Iller but even more than this, he endeavoured to acquire the Markgrafschaft Burgau and even the Palatinate Duchy Neuburg on the Danube. Anton Fugger took these negotiations extremely seriously. Despite setbacks, in 1546 the Fugger firm achieved its all-time highest level of assets and Anton Fugger was at the pinnacle of his wealth and power.

In 1546, there was no doubt that the major income was from Spain. Antwerp had become the second most important location for the Fugger business, even more than the Head Office in Augsburg. Here there were negotiations with the Tsars and with the King of Portugal, plans made for expansion to Sweden and for mining in Norway, intervention in the disputes over the Danish throne and in the election of a new pope in Rome. At this time Anton began to take money out of the business for investment in real estate. Times were overshadowed by war and religious disputes and were becoming insecure, at the same time the credit demands from the House of Habsburg were more and more persistent and their attitude to repayment worse. The relationship of the Fuggers to the Spanish government was also deteriorating.

In 1549, the Head of the Fugger concern was seriously considering the dissolution of the company. There was still no obvious successor to head the Fugger firm.

The Schmalkaldic War from 1546/47 was won by Charles V against the Protestant Princes only by means of credit granted by Anton Fugger to the amount of half a million florins. One of the losers of this war was Augsburg. In order to save his hometown from destruction, on 29th January 1547 Anton Fugger went down on his knees to the emperor. The old-established patricians of Augsburg would not have undertaken this symbolic gesture of subservience.

For the last time in 1552, Anton Fugger made his mark in world history: The revolt by the Protestant Prince Moritz von Sachsen, Count Wilhelm von Hessen and Margrave Albrecht-Alcibiades von Brandenburg caused Charles V to flee to Innsbruck. Here he wrote in despair to his banker: "Please come immediately—this is what I really want at this moment." When Anton Fugger arrived, they then together fled to Villachin Carinthia. Fugger once again granted a large loan which in fact meant that Charles V and the Habsburg Realm was saved yet again. In 1555, the "Freedom of Religion" Agreement was signed in Augsburg, an agreement between the confessions.

The end of the Fugger era

In 1556, Charles V abdicated. His successor, the Emperor Ferdinand I, who had never been a friend of the Fuggers anyway and Charles' son, Spain's new King Philipp II, regarded the Augsburg company not as a partner but only as a cow to be milked. New credit arrangements were forced through, promises were not kept, lies and deceit were the order of the day. In 1557, the Spanish declared state bankruptcy, and this cost the Fuggers a fortune. The "gratitude of the House of Habsburg" became a known saying.

Anton Fugger died on 14th September 1560 at the age of 67. For 35 years he had managed the "global business" of his Augsburg company. Anton wanted to be laid to rest in Babenhausen, not in Augsburg, where in the course of the Reformation the burial tombs of his ancestors in St. Moritz had been destroyed. With the death of Charles V and Anton Fugger, an epoch came to an end: The Age of the Fuggers.

Mexico
Veracruz
Santo Domingo
Santa Marta
Maracaibo
Coro
Portobelo
Nombre de Dios
Panama
Callao
Lima
Huancavelica
Chincha
Pacific
Potosi
Rio de Janeiro
Buenos Aires
Levantine connections to India
Fugger and Welser sea routes for East India trading
Fugger routes to America
Welser routes to America

Hamburg
London
Antwerpen
Augsburg
Genua
Venice
Madrid
Marseille
Lisbon
Barcelona
Sanlucár de Barrameda
Sevilla
Cádiz
Alexandrette
Aleppo
Ormuz
Cannanore
Goa
Cochin
Calicut
Quilon
Benin
Mombasa
Quiloa
Mosambik
Sofala
Atlantic
Indian Ocean
N
W
O
S

Much more than just memorials: The Fuggerei, castles and churches

1560 to the present: The Fuggers as landowners, founders and patrons

Two things were achieved by Anton Fugger beyond his death: Despite the bankruptcy of the Spanish state a large portion of the Fugger assets were retained because of investments he had made with thought to the future. For this reason the Fugger firm survived the years from 1556 to 1584, when in Augsburg alone, some 70 internationally renowned companies ended through bankruptcy.

When he set up a joint legally recognised organisation, Anton Fugger thus also ensured the continuation of his uncle Jakob Fugger's foundation to the present day. A joint Fugger Foundation Administration Board today manages the Fuggerei, the Fugger Chapel in the Anna Church and seven other foundations.

Of course it cannot be denied that the relationship of the Fuggers with the House of Habsburg would have brought further enormous losses. Five years after the bankruptcy of the Spanish state in 1557, Spain and the Fugger firm entered an agreement in respect of redemption of credits. The Augsburg Banking House was still much needed. In

Still today, the Fuggerei in Augsburg is a memorial to Jakob Fugger.

1575, there was in fact a second state bankruptcy, but by no means dissolving of the business relationship. There had always been a possibility of getting credit from the Fuggers and the Spanish King Philipp II and his administration were not very interested in the merits of the Fuggers vis-à-vis the Habsburgs. From the Spanish Chancellor Olivarez we know of the demand that the Bank House Fugger must sign a new credit agreement—"and even if in doing so this ruins the Fuggers".

But the Fuggers were not ruined, not even after a third bankruptcy of the Spanish State in 1607 which once again caused the Fugger firm enormous losses of well over one million florins. In 1626, the Spanish King forced the Fugger firm to accept his notes of indebtedness which were in fact now to a large extent worthless. In 1650, the Fuggers were forced out of Spanish business altogether. None of this however, and not even the Thirty Years' War, during which time from 1632 to 1634 Augsburg was said to have lost more than 60 percent of its population of 40,000 and its economic importance waned, could drive the Fugger company into bankruptcy. Their major competitors, the Welsers of Augsburg, did not do so well and went bankrupt in 1614.

The Fugger company was deemed to be at an end with the closure of the Tyrol ore trade in 1657 and 1658. In 1625, the Fuggers were still amongst the top six major tax payers in Augsburg but their payments had substantially decreased because much of their estate had already gone to heirs in the country.

In the Augsburg Fugger house: A box full of gold

The legendary splendour of the Fuggers was never forgotten. In 1575, a traveller to the Fugger House in Augsburg wrote: "Mr. Fugger kept a treasury of chains, small treasures, jewels and precious stones together with rare coins and gold pieces of such size that he himself said it was worth more than a million. He then opened a box full of golden ducats and florins."

When the Swedes occupied Augsburg during the Thirty Years' War, the Catholic Fuggers had long since withdrawn from their home town. The historian Franz Herre: "Land ownership provided security for various branches of the family: Kirchberg-Weissenhorn, Oberndorf-Nordendorf, Kirchheim-Gloett-Mickhausen, Babenhausen-Boos-Wellenburg. They

The Fuggerei is the most famous tourist attraction in Augsburg. VIP visitors such as the former Russian Head of State Michail Gorbatschow are often welcomed on a tour of this social settlement.

were landowners, builders, patrons of the arts and lovers of music...".

The historian Robert Mandrou wrote: "... in principle they did not sell any real estate or land once this had come into their possession...". Although they found themselves in-between Habsburg and Wittelsbach territories, nevertheless the Fuggers managed to acquire the "greatest complex of territorial rule in east Swabia" after Oettingen county. From the beginning of the 16th century until 1618 some 633 acquisitions are documented as Fugger purchases–including land, labourers' houses, forests, meadows, lakes and waterways.

Traces of the Fuggers can still be found today not only in Augsburg, but also in many parts of Bavaria, some areas of eastern Baden-Wurttemberg, and in many countries of Europe. The name Fugger became synonymous with "the obligation of supporting art and artists, a high level of patronage and a grandiose way of life". The Fuggers were patrons to highranking musicians of Europe. The Fugger foundations created or embellished many churches of the Renaissance, baroque or rococo eras.

In 1944, in the course of World War II, air raids caused substantial damage to the Fuggerei, the Fugger Chapel and the Fugger Houses.

Today the Augsburg Fuggerei is a world-renowned destination for tourists from around the world. The story of the social settlement (also in English) is told in and by the Fugger museum, the air raid shelter in the Fuggerei as well as numerous information panels located on buildings.

After 1945 these were rebuilt and restored. The social settlement was further extended, the last time in 1973.

Members of the Fugger family have entered history books as town aldermen, military campaigner, prince bishops, freedom fighters or parliamentarians. Up to the present day, members of the Fugger family are counted amongst the leading families of Germany. Their most important memorials today can be found in and around the city of Augsburg, also known as "The Fuggerstadt". But even more important than the castles and churches is the world famous social settlement founded by Jakob Fugger the Rich for poor citizens of Augsburg: The Fuggerei.

The Fugger tour leads to attractions in the Fugger city Augsburg with 15 information panels (also in English).

Jakob Fugger
genannt „Der Reiche“

Sightseeing in Augsburg: The Fuggers

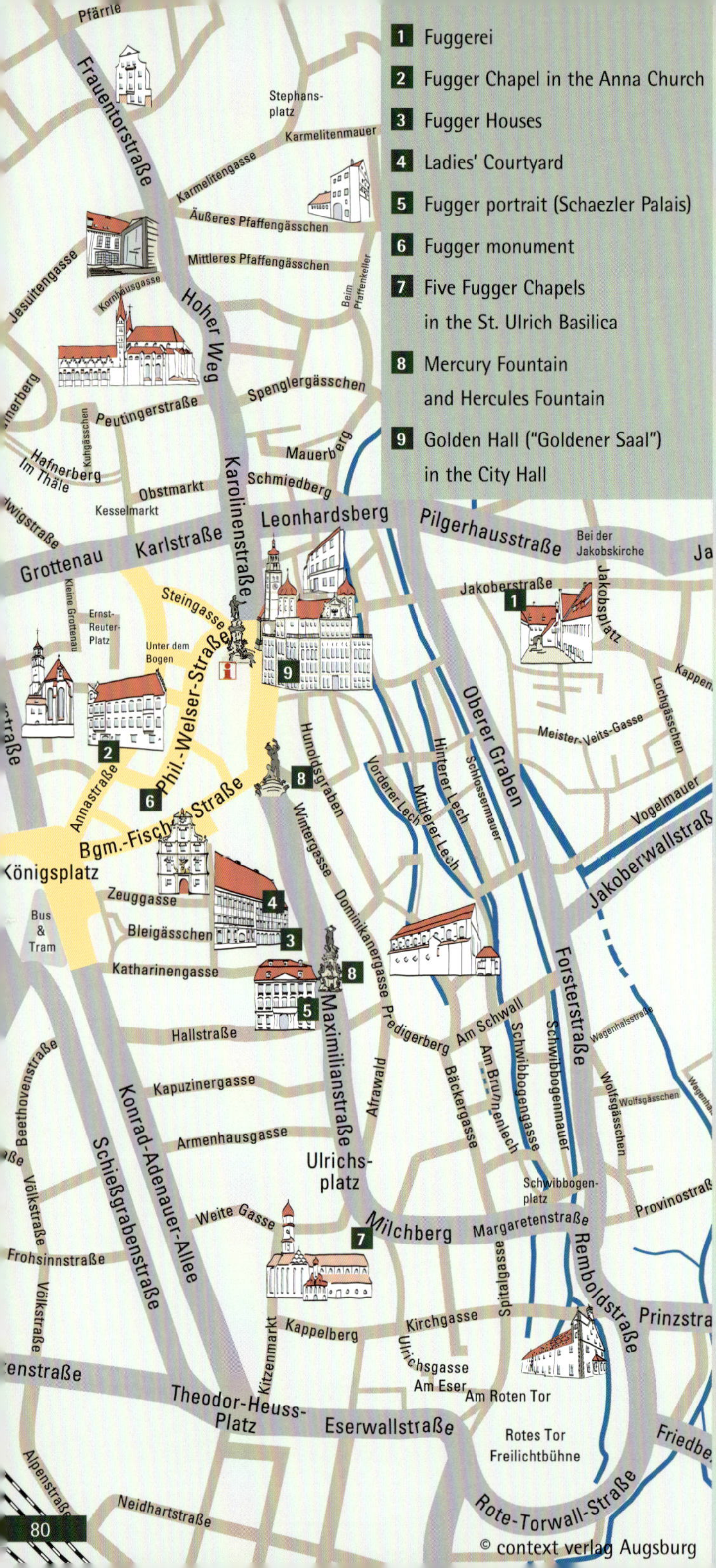

1 Fuggerei
2 Fugger Chapel in the Anna Church
3 Fugger Houses
4 Ladies' Courtyard
5 Fugger portrait (Schaezler Palais)
6 Fugger monument
7 Five Fugger Chapels in the St. Ulrich Basilica
8 Mercury Fountain and Hercules Fountain
9 Golden Hall ("Goldener Saal") in the City Hall
Pfärrle
Frauentorstraße
Stephansplatz
Karmelitenmauer
Karmelitengasse
Äußeres Pfaffengässchen
Mittleres Pfaffengässchen
Beim Pfaffenkeller
Jesuitengasse
Kornhausgasse
Hoher Weg
Spenglergässchen
Peutingerstraße
Kuhgässchen
Hafnerberg
Im Thäle
Mauerberg
Schmiedberg
Obstmarkt
Kesselmarkt
Karolinenstraße
Leonhardsberg
Pilgerhausstraße
Bei der Jakobskirche
Karlstraße
Grottenau
Kleine Grottenau
Ernst-Reuter-Platz
Steingasse
Unter dem Bogen
Jakoberstraße
Jakobsplatz
Phil.-Welser-Straße
Hunoldsgraben
Oberer Graben
Meister-Veits-Gasse
Lochgässchen
Schlossermauer
Hinterer Lech
Vorderer Lech
Mittlerer Lech
Annastraße
Bgm.-Fischer-Straße
Wintergasse
Vogelmauer
Jakoberwallstraße
Königsplatz
Zeuggasse
Bleigässchen
Bus & Tram
Katharinengasse
Dominikanergasse
Forsterstraße
Predigerberg
Am Schwall
Schwibbogengasse
Schwibbogenmauer
Am Brunnenlech
Wagenhalsstraße
Wolfsgässchen
Hallstraße
Maximilianstraße
Afrawald
Bäckergasse
Beethovenstraße
Kapuzinergasse
Armenhausgasse
Konrad-Adenauer-Allee
Schießgrabenstraße
Völkstraße
Ulrichsplatz
Schwibbogenplatz
Provinostraße
Weite Gasse
Milchberg
Margaretenstraße
Frohsinnstraße
Spitalgasse
Remboldstraße
Prinzstraße
Kappelberg
Kirchgasse
Kitzenmarkt
Ulrichsgasse
Am Eser
Am Roten Tor
Theodor-Heuss-Platz
Eserwallstraße
Rotes Tor Freilichtbühne
Alpenstraße
Neidhartstraße
Rote-Torwall-Straße

Sightseeing in Augsburg:
From the Fuggerei to the Fugger Chapel

Where the interesting places of the "German Medici" can be found

The Fugger family was called the "German Medici" by the Reformer Philipp Melanchthon because of their riches coupled with their love of art. Many commemorations of the arts in the "Golden Augsburg of the Renaissance" and the great Age of the Fuggers can soon be discovered on a short walk from the Fuggerei, the world famous Jakob Fugger monument, to the St. Ulrich Basilica at the southern end of the Maximilian Strasse.

On the way, for example, is the Fugger Chapel, the Fugger monument, the Fugger Houses and the Ladies' Courtyard or the famous portrait of Jakob Fugger, created by Albrecht Dürer of Nuremberg.

The following places of interest are listed in the order in which they are seen on the left hand side of the city map. In and around Augsburg there are further destinations well worth a visit in the traces of the Fugger dynasty.

Jakob Fugger (centre), painted on the organ in the Fugger Chapel.

A central point: Every visitor passes by the "Schalenbrunnen", the fountain in the Fuggerei.

1 The Fuggerei

Jakob Fugger the Rich founded the Fuggerei in 1521 as a social settlement for needy citizens of Augsburg. The annual rent (excluding heating) for an apartment is still the nominal value of one Rhine guilder (currently 0.88 euros) as well as three prayers per day for the founder and the Fugger family. Presently 150 persons occupy 140 apartments in 67 buildings. The most prominent resident of the Fuggerei was the master builder Franz Mozart, the great-grandfather of the composer Wolfgang Amadeus Mozart.

At the entrance gate to the Fuggerei there is a plaque with an inscription in commemoration of the founders of the social settlement.

The Fuggerei today is the oldest social settlement in the world. It is not only unique in age, but also in continuity: The social settlement is still financed exclusively through an endowment. And still today, the conception is considered exemplary. The Fuggerei is not only a shining example of architecture now as it also was in the past. The concept was already

groundbreaking nearly 500 years ago: Jakob Fugger did not allow residents to become paupers, but rendered assistance for self-help. With this concept, the founder was much ahead of the demands made by Reformer Martin Luther and later Catholic social reformers.

The Fuggerei, an ensemble with eight lanes and seven gates, is a "city within a city" having its own church, "city walls" and "city gates". Inscribed plaques over three gates and the stone lily coat of arms serve as reminders of the founding family. Especially important sights are the Fugger museum (entrance Mittlere Gasse 14, the front of the house is marked with a plaque commemorating the great-grandfather of Wolfgang Amadeus Mozart), the Markus church at "Markusplätzle" as well as the Hoechstetter Oriel on

View of the Mittlere Gasse of the Fuggerei. This is the way to the new Fuggerei Museum.

The Hoechstetter Oriel is from the town residence of an Augsburg family who were competitors of the Fugger family. It was re-erected on the administration building in the Jakober Strasse after World War II.

Historic rooms in the Fuggerei Museum show life in the Fuggerei 200 years ago.

the administrative building on Jakoberstrasse.

The Fuggerei museum displays the lifestyle of earlier times in three rooms found in the only apartment of the Fuggerei which has been preserved in its original condition. In 2006 a modern didactic area of the museum was newly opened where the story of the Fuggers and the Fuggerei is documented on film, with text and picture boards as well as with exhibits.

Illustrations, exhibitions and a film inform visitors to the Fuggerei Museum about the history of the social settlement.

The model apartment at Ochsengasse 51 shows the current lifestyle of Fuggerei residents. The unoccupied fully furnished apartment at Ochsengasse 51 displays the lifestyle of Fuggerei residents today. A TV set showing a documentary film conveys the story of the Fuggers.

Shortly after World War II began, an air raid shelter was erected in the Fuggerei. Here a permanent exhibition entitled "The Fuggerei in World War II–Destruction and Reconstruction" shows the fate of the Fuggerei and its residents

during the time of National Socialism and in the phase of post-war reconstruction. Texts and photographs, film and sound as well as exhibits all document the bombing of Augsburg during World War II plus the reconstruction of both the Fuggerei and the city of Augsburg.

Inscriptions on fronts define the present or past functions of the

The Fuggerei air raid shelter documents the destruction of the social settlement during World War II.

The museum apartment shows how the residents of the Fuggerei live today.

buildings and offer astonishing details as well. A monument to founder Jakob Fugger can be located in the park of the Fuggerei.

A little Fuggerei shop ("Fuggerei-Lädle") is the museum shop of the Fuggerei with souvenirs and literature about the Fuggers, the Fuggerei and Augsburg. Here you will find a small café and, weather permitting, a beer garden full of atmosphere.

Fuggerei
Jakober Strasse (Entrance)
Open April – September
8 a.m. till 8 p.m.,
October – March
9 a.m. till 6 p.m.
Phone ++ 49 (0) 8 21/31 98 81-0

8
7
5
2
4
3
1

1 Entrance gate on the Jakober Strasse
2 Administration Building
3 Hoechstetter Oriel
4 Senior Council Building
5 St. Mark's Church
6 Schalen Fountain
7 Fuggerei Museum
8 Commemorative plaque for Franz Mozart
9 Fuggerei Souvenir Shop
10 Museum apartment
11 Fuggerei air raid shelter

Jakob Fugger and his two brothers were buried in the Fugger Chapel in the Anna Church.

2 Fugger Chapel in the Anna Church

The Fugger Chapel, designed by Albrecht Dürer and erected between 1509 and 1512 in the St. Anna Church is deemed to be the first and most perfect Renaissance structure in Germany. It was donated by the brothers Ulrich, Georg and Jakob Fugger. It is said that Albrecht Dürer planned the Fugger Chapel. Other famous artists of the time were involved in the design.

The crypt of the Fugger Chapel is under the burial chapel beneath the precious marble floor where the Fugger lily and the Fugger trademark (trident with ring) can be seen. On the organ wing paintings (first created in 1512, today a reproduction) by Hans Breu the Elder, there is also a painting of Jakob Fugger the Rich. The epitaphs for Ulrich and Georg Fugger were designed in accordance with sketches by Albrecht Dürer. A curiosity: The catholic Jakob Fugger and his brothers Ulrich and Georg, as well as his two nephews Raymund and Hieronymus, were all buried in this church which became a Protestant church after 1525 (with short interruptions).

On the other side, in the east chancel hangs a portrait of Martin Luther painted by Lukas Cranach the Elder in 1529. The monk of Wittenberg was one of the most vigorous critics of the Fugger company, its business transactions and monopolies. In 1518, Luther the Reformer was interrogated in the nearby Fugger Houses by the Papal Legate, Cardinal Cajetan, on the grounds of his theses. Shortly afterwards, Luther fled from Augsburg. Commemoration of the Reformation in Augsburg can be found in the so-called "Lutherstiege" (Luther's Stairs) in the Church of St. Anna: Here there are exhibits and information charts about Luther and on the history of the Reformation in Augsburg.

3 Fugger Houses

Jakob Fugger the Rich commissioned the building of the Fugger Houses in 1512. After their de-

Once the headquarters of a global business power: The Augsburg Fugger Houses on Maximilian Strasse. Today used as business premises, including the Fuerst Fugger Private Bank.

struction during World War II, Prince Carl Fugger-Babenhausen had the buildings all rebuilt as they were.

Memorial plaques on the house wall remind us that the Fugger business empire was managed from here and that in 1518 the Reformer Martin Luther was interrogated by Cardinal Cajetan. In the center of the front façade is the so-called "Adlertor" (Eagle Gate), which indicates that the Fugger Houses also provided accommodation to the Emperor. The Fugger Houses, with the exception of three inner courtyards, are not accessible to the public.

Two of the courtyards which can be visited are the Ladies' Courtyard and the Serenade Courtyard. Here on the north side is the white oriel, a bay window, behind which were the magnificent chambers of the Emperor Charles V. A Fugger coat of arms decorates the rear portal of this Fugger House in the Zeugplatz. This was the area of the former Fugger concert hall, in which Wolfgang Amadeus Mozart once gave a legendary concert in 1777. The Fugger city palace is today under the ownership of the Princes Fugger-Babenhausen.

The first non-sacred building of the Renaissance in Germany: The Ladies' Courtyard in the Fugger Houses.

4 Ladies' Courtyard

This magnificent courtyard within the Fugger Houses is regarded as one of the most beautiful courtyards in Germany and as the first non-sacred building north of the Alps to be erected in Italian Renaissance style. Jakob Fugger the Rich commissioned its construction between 1512 and 1515. To get to the Ladies' Courtyard, (Damenhof) access is via the small so-called "Ladies' Maids' Courtyard" (Zofenhof).

5 Fugger portrait by Albrecht Dürer

In "The State Gallery of Old German Masters" in the former St. Catherine's Church on Maximilian Strasse is the painting by Albrecht Dürer of his patron and client Jakob Fugger the Rich (around 1518). Access to the permanent exhibits of the Gallery of Old German Masters and the main center for the "Art Collections of Augsburg" with a number of collections is through Augsburg's Schaezler Palais, a rococo city palace.

Dürer's portrait of Jakob Fugger is on view at the State Gallery of Old German Masters.

6 The Fugger Monument

The Fugger monument in Philippine-Welser-Strasse represents Hans Jakob Fugger. He was an art-loving collector and in 1571 sold his valuable collection of antique manuscripts and books to the Court at Munich. These volumes form the core of the Bavarian State Library. In 1857, King Ludwig I of Bavaria donated the more than life-size bronze statue of Hans Jakob Fugger who was a member of the Council of Munich and who became Court Chamber President.

The monument to Hans Jakob Fugger, a donation from a king of Bavaria.

7 Five Fugger chapels in the Basilica of St. Ulrich

In the Basilica of St. Ulrich, the second largest church in Augs-

The Chapel of St. Andrew is one of the five Fugger tombs in the St. Ulrich Basilica.

burg, there are five Fugger burial chapels, furnished like the tombs of princes with valuable works of art, epitaphs and the Fugger coat of arms. The Fugger organ, an integral part of one of the Fugger chapels, was once played (in 1777) by Wolfgang Amadé Mozart. The original instrument is no longer preserved but the two painted wings are original. Above the organ, angels with the Fugger coat of arms commemorate the founders.

8 Mercury Fountain and Hercules Fountain

Two of the three magnificent fountains in the Maximilian Strasse were planned and built during the time that the Alderman Octavian Secundus Fugger was in office. The Mercury Fountain was erected from 1596 to 1599 according to designs by Adriaen de Vries, who also designed the Hercules Fountain during this time after 1596.

9 The Golden Hall

The power and wealth of Augsburg during the Fugger era are also reflected in the breath-taking splendour of the "Goldener Saal" in the Renaissance town hall of Augsburg (built in 1615 to 1620 by Elias Holl). Frescoes of great imperial rulers decorate its walls, including Charles V, who became emperor in 1519 with the aid of

The name Fugger can also be found in the magnificent „Goldener Saal" of the Augsburg town hall.

money from the Fugger family. One of the principals for the construction of the town hall was also Johannes Fugger, whose name is immortalized in a commemorative plaque above the south portal.

Fugger castles around Augsburg

There are still members of the Fugger family living here today. Representatives of the three branches of the family live in castles in the Augsburg area. The Fugger Museum at the Castle of Babenhausen and the Cedar Hall at Kirchheim Castle are certainly interesting to visit.

The Fugger Castle of Wellenburg

Wellenburg has been in existence since the 13th century. Since 1595 this castle has belonged to the Fugger family, since 1764 in the hands of the Babenhausen line of the Fugger dynasty. A well-known previous occupant was the Emperor Maximilian I, who had built a castle here in 1507. There is no public access to Wellenburg Castle.

The Fugger Castle of Wellenburg.

Anton Fugger had Babenhausen Castle built in Allgaeu. Today it houses the Fugger museum.

The Fugger Castle Babenhausen

In 1538, Anton Fugger purchased this castle which had existed since 1237 and in 1541 had it completely restored and converted. The complex of various buildings, including the Rechberg building, the "New Castle", the west wing, the chancellery and various farm buildings, is principally grouped around two courtyards. The Fugger Museum in the west wing and in the New Castle has an exhibition of over 500 years of Fugger family and Fugger company history. On a guided tour of the Ancestral Hall in the new castle you can see portraits of numerous members of this dynasty from the 16th and 17th century. The castle grounds are open to the public during the normal opening times. Anton Fugger's epitaph can be seen in the castle chapel.

The Fugger Castle Kirchheim

In 1551, Anton Fugger purchased the small market town of Kirchheim near to the town of Mindelheim together with the castle there. His son Hans had a magnificent new building constructed in 1578 to 1582 which contemporaries compared with the palace of the king of Spain and it thus came to be called the "Escorial of Swabia". The "Cedar Hall" with its fine panelled ceiling made in 1585 is 30 meters long, 12 meters wide and 10 meters high. This, as also the castle park, can be viewed during opening times. The family crypt of Hans Fugger can be seen in the castle chapel. The marble tomb shows the builder of this castle as a life-size recumbent figure in full armorial splendour. A few steps away there is a painting which could well be by Rubens.

The Fugger Castle in Kirchheim in Allgaeu.

The Fugger Castle Oberkirchberg

In 1507, Jakob Fugger acquired administration rights to the town of Weissenhorn together with rule

The Castle of Oberkirchberg was purchased by Jakob Fugger in the year 1507.

of Kirchberg with its castle, which was the gateway to Ulm. This Fugger castle, located to the west of the River Iller (already in the State of Baden-Wurttemberg) was converted to its present form after 1750. The building complex is grouped around a courtyard, with access via a gate erected in 1763. Above this gateway is a very impressive alliance coat of arms showing the Fugger lily.

The Fugger town of Weissenhorn is only a few minutes by car from the Oberkirchberg. Here there are two former Fugger castles. In this region there are still a number of well-preserved Fugger castles.

Fugger churches around Augsburg

There are still numerous Fugger churches to be found today in the area around Augsburg. Sacred buildings with a Fugger history are only a few minutes away from Augsburg by car.

St. Jakob in Biberbach

Biberbach and the nearby Castle Markt were purchased by Jakob Fugger in the year 1514. In 1766, initiated by Christoph Moritz Graf Fugger, there was a church organ competition in the St. Jakob Church of Pilgrimage in Biberbach on 6th November 1766 and two child prodigies took part: The ten-year-old Mozart competed against the local boy Sigmund Eugen Bachmann. According to a chronicler of the time there was no clear winner.

St. Ulrich and Afra in Graben

The Fugger family originated from the village of Graben to the south of Augsburg, according to the family legend of the Fuggers. In the parish church of St. Ulrich and Afra there is a half-length portrait in commemoration of the merchant Hans Fugger who migrated to Augsburg in 1367.

Portrait of Hans Fugger, who migrated to Augsburg in 1367, in the church in Graben.

The Fugger family donated this memorial to the founder of their dynasty in 1898.

Thekla Church in Welden

Count Joseph Maria Fugger of Wellenburg founded this church in 1756. In the interior of this jewel of rococo style is a life-size image of its founder: The north founder altar shows the founder kneeling before St. Thekla. The Fugger coat of arms and symbols

The Thekla Church in Welden was built till 1758.

of previous history are found on the southern founder altar. Count Joseph Maria Fugger was laid to rest here.

St. Wolfgang in Mickhausen

Around 1535 the Fuggers built a castle and a church of St. Wolfgang in Mickhausen. In the sacral building is a Fugger crypt. Precious glass windows commemorate the founder Raymund Fugger and the Habsburgs.

Glass window in the village church of Mickhausen showing the Fugger coat of arms.

The Maria Geburt Church in Witzighausen

The Fugger family funded the erection of this elaborate baroque church of pilgrimage near Ulm, completed in 1740. The Fugger coat of arms can be seen above the chancel and at the entrance to the Parsonage.

The baroque church of pilgrimage in Witzighausen, commissioned by the Fuggers.

Maria Himmelfahrt in Kirchhaslach

From the outside the Maria Himmelfahrt Church in Kirchhaslach looks quite modest. With former Fugger patronage it is in fact a jewel of the baroque, with an extremely elaborate interior including stucco, a pietà and a monumental painting "The Ascension of Maria" above the high altar.

One of the most important Fugger churches in Allgaeu: The church of Kirchhaslach.

Pictures by courtesy of

Title:

Wolfgang B. Kleiner

Photos on back cover:

Martin Kluger (2), Wolfgang B. Kleiner (2)

Photos in the book:

Ulrich M. Alexander: 69

Thomas, Baumgartner: 53, 54, 57, 60, 64, 65, 67, 68, 81 (1), 95 (1)

context verlag Augsburg: 8 (1), 14 (1), 40/41, 42, 44/45, 55, 82 (1), 86/87

Fürst Fugger Privatbank: 12 (1)

Holweg, Gerhard: 24 (1), 51

Wolfgang B. Kleiner: 1, 2/3, 5 (3), 6/7, 8/9, 10/11, 10 (1), 14/15, 16 (1), 22/23, 26/27, 30/31, 30 (1), 32 (2), 34/35, 36/37, 36 (2), 46 (1), 47 (1), 52, 59, 61, 70, 74, 77 (1), 78/79, 81 (1), 82 (1), 83 (1), 84 (2), 89 (1), 90 (1), 94 (1), 95 (1)

Hannah Kluger: 24/25, 46 (1)

Martin Kluger: 8 (1), 10 (1), 12/13, 12 (1), 14 (1), 16/17, 16 (1), 18/19, 18 (2), 20 (2), 22 (2), 24 (1), 26 (2), 28/29, 28 (1), 30 (1), 32/33, 34 (2), 38/39, 38 (2), 43, 47 (1), 50, 56, 58, 66, 76, 77 (1), 83 (1), 85 (2), 88, 89 (1), 90 (1), 91 (2), 92 (2), 93 (2), 94 (1), 95 (1)

Manfred Lehnerl: 28 (1)

Regio Augsburg Tourismus GmbH: 20/21